ZODIAC

DENBIGHSHIRE

Edited by Simon Harwin

First published in Great Britain in 2002 by
YOUNG WRITERS
Remus House,
Coltsfoot Drive,
Peterborough, PE2 9JX
Telephone (01733) 890066

All Rights Reserved

Copyright Contributors 2002

HB ISBN 0 75433 528 3
SB ISBN 0 75433 529 1

FOREWORD

Young Writers was established in 1991 with the aim of promoting creative writing in children, to make reading and writing poetry fun.

Once again, this year proved to be a tremendous success with over 41,000 entries received nationwide.

The Zodiac competition has shown us the high standard of work and effort that children are capable of today. The competition has given us a vivid insight into the thoughts and experiences of today's younger generation. It is a reflection of the enthusiasm and creativity that teachers have injected into their pupils, and it shines clearly within this anthology.

The task of selecting poems was a difficult one, but nevertheless, an enjoyable experience. We hope you are as pleased with the final selection in *Zodiac Denbighshire* as we are.

CONTENTS

Howell's School

	Emily Gardner	1
	Kate Jones	2
	Rebecca Clewarth	3
	Margaret Leanne Ord	4
	Sarah Thompson	6
	Anna Lindsay	7
	Sophie Williams	8
	Kirsty Jones	9
	Rose Pearson	10
	Laura Melling	11
	Lauren Oldbury	12
	Ruth Evans	13
	Katie Hawksworth	14
	Lauren Wynne-Williams	15
	Niveditha Muthukumar	16
	Abigail New	17
	Joyce Chan	18

Ruthin School

	Tom Roberts	19
	Jenny Lee	20
	Thomas Morris	21
	Tom Jenkins	22
	Charlotte Cumming	23
	Jonathan Andrews	24
	Lewys Jones	25
	Christine Hamilton-Rice	26
	Shiran Devakumar	27
	Richard Manley	28
	Jack Evans	29
	Natalie Roberts	30
	Lloyd Frith	31
	Louis Gibson	32
	Hannah Hughes	33
	Sam Ashton	34

	Oliver Soden	35
	Sioned Roberts	36
	Michael Manktelow	37
	Elisabeth Moore	38
	Toby Palmer-Speight	39
	Zac Davidson	40
	Adam Wynne	41
	Rhian Jones	42
	Marc Jones	43
	Thomas Moore	44
	Joseph Scott	45
	Hugh Dixon	46
Ysgol Brynhyfryd		
	Berwyn Eyton Jones	47
	Wiliam Joseff Davies	48
	Louise Francis	49
	Elan Evans	50
	Siôn Owen	51
	Ffiona Mair Jones	52
	Ceri Eagle	53
	Beca Haf Parry	54
	Daniel Brixey	56
	Sam Shillito	57
	Eilir Wyn Roberts	58
	Clwyd Edwards	59
	Alan Armstrong	60
	Sioned Roberts	61
	Iestyn Jones	62
	Wil Sharp	63
	Emily Freeman	64
	Charlotte Masters	66
	Emma Braid	67
	Sara Bowler	68
	Becky Challinor	69
	Ben Mcleod	70
	Ffion Medi	71
	Huw Woodward	72

Owen Mills	73
Mathew Edge	74
Tom Potter	75
Robert Steffan Parry	76
Elin Morgan	77
Bethan Rowlands	78
Heledd Fflur Morgan	79
Lowri Stubbs	80
Cathryn Jones	81
Emma Jones	82
Lauren Gledhill	83
Jane Hesketh	84

Ysgol Dinas Brân

Zara Blain	85
Timothy Knibbs	86
Philip Pybus	87
Joanne Morris	88
Adam Rogers	90
Kay Rowley	91
Alex Bebbington	92
Nakita Furmage	93
William Eastwood	94
Susie Davies	95
Bethan Richards	96
Emma Watson	97
Natalie Astle	98
Paul Brown	99
Lee Jones	100
Hannah Green	101
Geraint Lloyd	102
Amy May Derbyshire-Styles	103
Holly Cottrell	104
Luke Smith	105
Dawn Morrison	106

Ysgol Emrys Ap Iwan
- Nicola Fleck — 107
- Jamie Blythin — 108
- Samantha Strauch — 109
- Louise Kirk — 110
- Jessica Whitehouse — 112
- James Longden — 113
- Stephen Marsh — 114
- Hannah Watson — 115
- Jazmine Bonnell — 116
- Daniel Constanzo — 117
- Christine Brough — 118
- Kieran Buser Evans — 119
- Liam Doyle — 120

The Poems

THE LAST WAVE GOODBYE

On a normal Tuesday morning when the streets are busy and loud,
People prepare for the workday ahead to make their families proud.
Paper, folders and cases are ready for the day that's breaking,
Lovers hold hands and kiss goodbye and greet the day awaking.

Fathers hug their children and kiss goodbye to their wives,
Everyone is busy going about their lives.
The lights are bright, the computers are on,
The calm and peaceful night-time is gone . . .

The birds fly all around, on a bright blue sunny day,
Some people look up when they hear a sound, a sound from far away.
A distant plane is swooping low and many heads turn to stare,
Buildings lie in the path of the plane, every soul is well aware.

The plane hasn't stopped and the tension is rising high,
The plane is deliberately off its course and hopes are beginning to die.
The plane is going to hit, nothing can be done,
People start to trip and jump and fall as they run.

Many have jumped from windows but not survived the fall,
The building is strong and firm but the walls are built too tall.
People try and try to escape the hitting plane,
But inside for many, their efforts are in vain.

The plane has hit, the place has fallen,
Years of work lie upon the ground,
Families cry out for fear of their loved ones not ever being found.
The hope for survivors is looking weak,
Many walk around unwilling to speak.

Lives have been ruined, families drawn apart,
Loved ones are suffering from a broken heart.
Things will never be the same,
Not now, not ever, not ever again.

Emily Gardner (13)
Howell's School

THE JOURNEY

The dazzling sun appeared
As the clouds instantly vanished,
A fresh breeze stretched out across the land,
And all was serene and quiet.

The vibrant flowers frolicked in the breeze,
As the variegated trees swayed to and fro.
The grass was glimmering in the heat,
In the air, scented of pollen.

The birds emerged to sing and waltz
In the baby blue coloured sky,
Why can't days like this last forever?
Why
   Oh
      Why
         Oh
           Why?

Kate Jones (13)
Howell's School

The House On The Hill

The house stands on the hill,
Isolated from all that disturbs.
Where it dwells
There are no burdens.
Just beauty for miles on end.
Surrounded by hills and mountains,
Where predicaments don't exist.
It is forever peaceful,
And looks forever quaint.
No matter what problems you have
No matter how feeble you feel
The house on the hill is still perfect,
And able to calm your fears.
If there was ever a place that stopped time,
A place that witnessed everything around
This house would be it,
This house on a hill.

Rebecca Clewarth (13)
Howell's School

A FATEFUL FLIGHT

I think of all you've put us through,
I don't know how you could do it,
To ruin the lives of three people,
And say you would still have flew it.

Over the Atlantic we went,
Waves tumbling tenderly over each other,
Reflecting the early autumn sun,
Together we went, me, you, Johny and Mother.

The weather became tempestuous,
And the sky grew dismal and dark,
The waves increased in power and size,
And I swear I spotted a shark.

The lightning came and yet you still flew,
Then a colossal thunder clash,
The fateful images that went through my head,
When the danger light began to flash.

The plane started to spin perilously,
But still you kept your calm,
There was only one life jacket,
To save us all from harm.

The doors of the plane flew open,
You grabbed the life jacket and jumped,
The plane continued to plummet,
And in the ocean we were dumped.

They rescued you in a helicopter,
But us they did not find,
You carried on without a thought,
For those you left behind.

But now I'm back to haunt you,
I'm with you constantly,
Your selfishness killed me that night,
And I'll never set you free.

Margaret Leanne Ord (13)
Howell's School

HECTIC PEACE

I see a green sea,
I see white horses galloping towards me,
Yet it is calm.

I see an orange fire,
I see red, yellow and orange flames licking wood,
Yet it is still.

I see a blue pool,
It has black ripples waving across it,
Yet it is smooth.

This is my world,
As I see it on this autumn morning,
From the top of my hill.
It is busy and hectic,
Yet it is tranquil.

Sarah Thompson (13)
Howell's School

4000 AD: VOICE OF THE EARTH

'I gave them everything I had,
And made it free to all -
　But they've ruined it now:

I grew forests full of life,
Which were essential for my eco system -
　But they've felled them just for money.

I moved my crust around,
And filled the gaps with seas -
　But they've polluted the waters with waste.

I mixed and matched my scenery,
Which created awesome landscapes -
　But they've built towns there now.

To walk on my ground were animals,
Most with special features -
　But they've been hunted for their parts.

There were other creatures too,
Like birds and fish and more -
　But contamination's 'dealt' with them.

I won't forget my atmosphere,
It brought rain and wind and snow -
　But now it's all unclean.

To protect them from the sun,
I wore a layer of ozone -
　But even that has holes.

Why are they like this?
It's not like I haven't tried; I am gone now -
　But I can't even rest in peace.'

Anna Lindsay (13)
Howell's School

TERRORISTS

Early one morning all was fine,
The Earth was calm, there was no sign.
There was a noise so very loud,
Which disturbed the people in the crowd.
People screamed for help they needed,
Out of windows they waved and pleaded.
Even though help was on the way,
Another noise came to stay.
Everyone stared so scared and shocked,
All of a sudden the buildings rocked.
And smoke and dust came crumbling down,
Covering the ground like an enormous gown.
People caught in this horrific attack,
Were killed by people with a soul of black.
But hope is still all around,
For the people who are being found.
Families have lost the ones they care,
The morning it happened they were not aware.
People will help from far and near,
Trying to be strong and not to fear.
Our prayers and thoughts we share each day,
And we hope the terrorists will go away.

Sophie Williams (13)
Howell's School

SORRY MUM

Sorry Mum but when you are out . . .
I bang the doors and scream *and shout*

I swing the cat round by its tail
And lock my sister in a jail

I smash all your plates on the kitchen wall
And made a big mess of the great big hall

I run around upon your broom
And break the pictures in your room

I know I have been such a disaster
I will be good now my leg's in plaster.

Kirsty Jones (12)
Howell's School

WHITE HORSES

The seagulls reeled above
The seals wallowed below
And the cormorants dived into the deep
Like black missiles.

The rocks waited, patiently
The wind danced, mischievously
And the waves shattered on the rocks
Like thin glass.

The clouds gathered, ominously
The creatures dispersed, frantically
And the sea charged towards the land
Like a million white horses.

Rose Pearson (13)
Howell's School

THE STORM

Bang went the balloon,
off went the lights,
flicker, flicker on again.

Smash went the tennis ball against the wall,
flash as I turned my light off,
on went my torch.

Over the creaky stairs,
up woke Mum,
on came the lights.

Crash as I dropped the torch,
flash went the torch as it touched the ground.

Rumble as Mum closed the window,
dash went the light as she closed the curtain.

Off went the storm far, far away!

    Goodnight.

Laura Melling (11)
Howell's School

FLOWERS

Daisies sway in the wind while bluebells sing.
Snowdrops are the first sight of spring
With white petals and stems short and green.
Daffodils are beautiful flowers: yellow, orange and cream.
Water lilies live on ponds or swim down streams.
Buttercups are meadow flowers
Known to tell us whether we like butter or not.
Pansies are all different colours,
My favourites are yellow and purple.
Roses are a romantic flower, all red and glittery.
Forget-me-not, like blue summer skies in the morning, so
                                          fresh and bright.

Lauren Oldbury (11)
Howell's School

THE SIGHT OF LAND

Ships and boats,
With people on,
Looking into the horizon,
For the sight of land.

The crashing of the waves,
The crinkle of the water,
And the relaxing sound of the sea water,
Runs through your head.

The birds in the smooth, fresh air,
Glide through the water,
And see the high hills of the land,
That is in sight.

The glisten on the water,
And the quick glints,
I make my day at sea the best.

And in the morning time,
The sun comes up,
And the birds sing to wake the sea up.

Ruth Evans (11)
Howell's School

PARADISE

Coconut, papaya and mangoes
Are as nice as fruit gets.
Munching them as the sun starts to set.
The water is calm
There is not a sound
Nor a cloud to be found
The ground is covered in sand
Rich, golden and shimmers in the light
But you cannot see this at night.

Katie Hawksworth (11)
Howell's School

STRANDED

I've landed here on a desert island
Its soft golden sands glistening in the sunlight,
The palm trees swaying in the breeze,
The sound of coconuts hitting one another;
Sounding like wind chimes,
The exotic birds, colours of all
And the sound of the waves crashing,
Sounding like the snores of a sleeping cat.
It makes me think that being stranded isn't so bad after all.

Lauren Wynne-Williams (11)
Howell's School

THE COLOUR OF PARADISE

The sky as blue as sapphires
And the sun is brilliant and vibrant
Glistening on the turquoise waters
Forming frothy lace necklaces
The sand as white as snow, glowing in the sun
Whilst the palm trees sway with the breeze
The exotic fruits and coconuts are tempted to fall
On the beach where children play
And, the beautiful, colourful fish
Frolic in the waters of the Caribbean
To the sound of laughter.

Is this the colour of paradise?

Niveditha Muthukumar (11)
Howell's School

WHAT IS THE MOON?

The moon is like a ball,
floating in the dark.

A white plate,
on a black tablecloth.

A football that's been
kicked up in the black dark sky.

White cream
sitting on a chocolate cake.

Abigail New (11)
Howell's School

THE AUTUMN LEAVES

The autumn leaves are gold, orange and red,
Over time I see them, I can't dare to go to bed.
From time to time, they descend the trees,
Begin in the cool autumn breeze.

The autumn leaves jumping, dancing and flying,
As my mind is turning.
The leaves are twisting at my crinkled feet,
Until they're swirling at the back of the seat.

The autumn leaves are oval, round and square,
As I watch each one tear.
The wind comes and hugs them tight,
They whirl up and up like a kite.

The autumn leaves rustling, crunching and crackling,
Since my house has been collapsing,
Forever it stays in my mind,
The autumn has been ever so kind.

Joyce Chan (13)
Howell's School

FEAR

Deep, unseeing eyes,
Staring into space,
Not blinking, for fear of missing,
Fear.

Adrenaline coursing, surging,
Flowing through your deep, pulsating veins,
Rushing to speed up your heart
Which is already bursting
Out of your chest,
Beating so fast that you can
Almost taste it,
Hear it driving on.

Your muscles ripple,
As you sense it drawing near,
You brace yourself
For the pounce.

Then it comes.

Not quick, but steadily weaving its way
Between the cells,
Burrowing its way deep into the
Soft, pink flesh of your arm.
But it disappears almost
As silently as it came,
You relax, until the next time.

Tom Roberts (15)
Ruthin School

EXISTING

You stand alone and waver once in a while
But not of any significance, not to me at least.
Then in the breeze you come alive and
As I stare, my eyes are transfixed by your hypnotic glare.
A hair floats on the breeze getting nearer and nearer,
There's a slight 'fizz' as a double helix shows itself
Then disappears, as though it never existed.

As the wind grows stronger, you get more frantic
And you get closer to the end . . .
Finally, with one short blow, you are gone,
Leaving nothing but a cloud and a scent to remind
                              of your existence.

Goodbye, until the next time a match is struck.

Jenny Lee (15)
Ruthin School

THE ROSE

The heart of a jewel, blood-red in the night,
Healing, changing from season to season,
Its red dress unfurls for the day ahead,
Dew hangs on its lips,
Lips that beg you to kiss it,
The heart of the rose lives on forever.

Thomas Morris (14)
Ruthin School

LOVE IS A ROPE

The two ends meet, willing to be joined
The knot tied gives security and unity
Tireless tensions it will take
And yet remain unbroken

Its smooth surface will fray
Leaving its rough reality
Unbroken regardless
Accepting this harshness

It gives support when needed
Loyal and strong throughout
Metal loops enforce this
And ensures its solidness

Only the stone-blunted blade
Will break the special band
The unity gone, the ends broken
They part, cut and ragged.

Tom Jenkins (15)
Ruthin School

LONGING

All alone,
Standing amongst the mourning of others,
Waiting to look a part of something,
On the outside I look happy,
Full of flourishing foliage.

Only stumps left of my ancestors,
My children grow in black pipes.

Then, light comes,
Colours start to show,
Others grow foliage,
Pushing their branches against me.
Once again there is a longing,
But now it's changed.
I long to be free amongst others,
My space now invaded,
Rosy cheeks brought out amongst us,
Strong and ripe we stand.

Then -
Our dreaded fate,
Cut up to suit,
Then left to go rotten,
When not so cute.

Charlotte Cumming (16)
Ruthin School

ALONE

The wind blows strongly
As I set sail across the sea,
I glance back at her
Standing, lonely on the shoreline,
I slowly wave then turn my head away.

I ask myself why I am leaving,
Leaving my family and friends,
I pull the sail in,
As the wind strength increases
I realise, I will really miss her.

I am going to start a new life,
I don't want to, but I have to,
Her figure slowly disappears in the distance
And I feel my eyes swelling,
I suddenly feel now, very alone.

We used to sail together,
Across the open sea,
But now it has all happened,
Times have changed,
For now I must leave her.

Jonathan Andrews (15)
Ruthin School

EFFORT

So much of my heart and soul I poured into that work,
Drip by drip and hour by hour I romanced with my labour of love,
I killed my canvas with blood, sweat and tears,
Until it flowed like the liquid fire of my creativity.

Without prompt I kept on working late into the night,
Working in a puddle of moonlight, spilt forth from my window,
Trying to improve upon my glamorous masterpiece,
And when I had finished I displayed my creation to you.

Expecting a triumphant fanfare of loving praise,
You spat on it, and with one harsh gesture my pride was shattered,
That was when I choked on my efforts,
I felt the sweet shining glaze as if it were a French pastry.

It stuck to the side of my throat and asphyxiated me,
Into a world of shattered dreams and stark realisations,
And then my dreams faded into obscurity and my goals became history,
My dreams and myself died alone and unrecognised.

Lewys Jones (15)
Ruthin School

HOPE

It's a dark night and the once echoing corridor
is blossoming with flames.
A lonely lady's body is transported through
accompanied by a flicker of hope.
The constant bubble of heat in a channel
of draughts.

Reaching the furthest plausible point, a window
is ajar,
And through it floats a breeze hosting
silent notes.
Hope flickers in a battle with the cold puff
but sustains its energy.

Frozen to maintain the only comfort in a dark world,
a storm arises.
The curtain billows and the cruel wind taunts
the flame of hope.
The war is won and security is lost, then
the resurrection of fear commences in a
cloud of spite.

Christine Hamilton-Rice (15)
Ruthin School

UNREQUITED LOVE

I am a hedgehog,
You wouldn't think it, all sharp and prickly,
I curl up into a ball, hiding my true feelings,
I'm so easily frightened.

I live in the undergrowth, to hide myself away.
A dark brown colour, I scurry along,
Whenever she comes near.
I love her so, why won't she ever know?

Shiran Devakumar (15)
Ruthin School

LEO

A roller coaster in the sky
Heavy rock music from a sports car
Rotting wood
Cold metal on the roller coaster
The juicy burger
I must be home by midnight
Leo will come again.

Richard Manley (11)
Ruthin School

BOLDER COASTER

Bolder coaster
The music blaring from the rides
The smell of burning rubber
I touch my friend's coat
The taste of lemonade in my mouth
I stay later and risk all.

Jack Evans (12)
Ruthin School

AQUARIUS AT THE FAIRGROUND

A loop the loop roller coaster,
People screaming on the ghost train,
The smell of sugary candyfloss,
Reaching out for a twenty pound note on the ground,
I can taste burning hot chips in my mouth,
I must be home by midnight,
Aquarius has decided to go home.

Natalie Roberts (11)
Ruthin School

PISCES AT THE FAIRGROUND

Charming, beautiful, friendly and kind,
A soft voice coming out of clown music,
A girl running towards me smelling of flowers,
Silky soft hair of someone,
Strawberry lipstick of a girl's lips,
I must be home by midnight,
Pisces feels warm in the arms of his new girlfriend.

Lloyd Frith (11)
Ruthin School

CANCER AT THE FAIRGROUND

Gigantic roller coaster
Shooting from the shooting game
Teddy bears
The warmth of a hot dog
I must be home by midnight
Cancer will risk it.

Louis Gibson (11)
Ruthin School

ARIES AT THE FAIRGROUND

A big roller coaster,
The brakes on the roller coaster,
The smell of burning,
The sugary candyfloss,
The smoke from the rides.
I must be home by midnight,
Aries will risk all for fun.

Hannah Hughes (11)
Ruthin School

CANCER AT THE FAIRGROUND

A log flume
People screaming
The smell of rubber burning
Touching the teddy I won
The taste of a hot dog from the hot dog stall
I must be home by midnight
Cancer will take a risk and stay with his friends.

Sam Ashton (12)
Ruthin School

AQUARIUS

An ice cream shop,
The splash of water rides,
The smell of burning hot dogs,
The feel of the air,
The taste of oil,
I must be home by midnight,
Aquarius is going to go home.

Oliver Soden (11)
Ruthin School

THE FAIRGROUND

The screeching of the metal on the rides
Smell of sweat from the nervous people around me
My friends shivering when I touch their shoulders
The taste of the candyfloss
I must be home by midnight
Gemini is going to take the risk.

Sioned Roberts (11)
Ruthin School

LIBRA

There's a comedy act with people constantly laughing
The smell of charcoal burning
I am touching hot food
The taste of the icy atmosphere
I must be home by midnight
Libra risks it and will talk himself out of trouble.

Michael Manktelow (12)
Ruthin School

LEO'S FIVE SENSES

Smelling fresh and clean
Her touch is soft, gentle and kind
Taste of the happiness in her loving heart
Sight to make you smile and laugh
Hearing what you have to say
A help to reach for your dream.

Elisabeth Moore (11)
Ruthin School

I AM THE SCORPION

I can taste the tension
I can smell the venom
Always looking to persuade people
I can hear rages ready to sting
I can touch the point of the tail.

Toby Palmer-Speight (11)
Ruthin School

SCORPIO

My touch so forceful it will enthral you
But beware of scorpion inside me, it tastes so strange
The smell of fear in my venom
The venom will enthral and give you passion
You may hear the venom in my tongue
You fear my forceful sting, beware.

Zac Davidson (11)
Ruthin School

ARIES

I can smell danger from far away
I can hear a storm coming my way
I can touch your heart each and every day
I can taste all the colours of the bright rainbow
I can see Jupiter, Uranus and Pluto.

Adam Wynne (11)
Ruthin School

ARIES

Hides confidence in every way possible,
Risks a lot for happiness,
Dark hair, very tall,
I like to be quick,
Not to stand above the rest,
Gullible and dynamic,
I am Aries and I like to have fun.

Rhian Jones (12)
Ruthin School

CAPRICORN

Tall and thin, hiding the plans
Very ambitious but patient to think
Opinions of how to improve yourself
Hates it when anything ever goes wrong
But likes to entice you into the plan
Beware though, for he could be sly.

Marc Jones (12)
Ruthin School

VIRGO

Black hair hides my shyness
I work hard to achieve my ambition
I like to tell people my opinions
I dislike Leos
I plan ahead to make my life easy
I am Virgo - hardworking and shy.

Thomas Moore (12)
Ruthin School

TAURUS

I look strong within myself and I am very ambitious,
I like people who look after you well,
I dislike people who think themselves brilliant,
My personality is stormy, I always try my hardest,
I think that evil should be driven to extinction,
I would like to do things with pride and help others.

Joseph Scott (12)
Ruthin School

I AM ARIES

Tall and blond, you will notice me,
My ambition, for never-ending money,
I am quick, but maybe too much for you,
Everything is worth anything, for me too,
I love to gamble for money and more,
For I am Aries, but beware,
There is such a thing as too much fun.

Hugh Dixon (12)
Ruthin School

FIRST DAY AT BRYNHYFRYD

Which way should I go?
What lesson have I got next?
I'm lost!
I get carried away by a wave of pupils,
And disappear under the green sea . . .
I somehow see yellow fishes,
That have three fins sticking out of their backs.
I finally get dropped off somewhere,
That I don't recognise.
I don't know where I am,
The bell must 'ave gone!
Oh no! Panic! Panic!
Where should I go?
The staff room of course.
Uh . . . where's that?
Or . . . the form room,
They must have gone there.
Oh . . . where was it again?
Oh! Where am I?
'You're in your bedroom,
Late for school young man!'
Mum! It was a dream.
I hope the real thing won't be like that.
I finally reach school.
Awfully quiet!
No one around!
Oh no!

Berwyn Eyton Jones (11)
Ysgol Brynhyfryd

SCHOOL

Gum under the tables and chairs,
Teachers shouting,
Girls shrieking,
Oh my pen's leaking.

Time passes slowly waiting for the bell,
Can't someone save me from this hell?
Moving onto the next block.
Time for English and maths
According to the clock.

English, maths, history, geog,
Oh what a slog!
Teachers going on and on but no one cares,
French lesson next, up the stairs.

The Battle of Hastings,
Just isn't for me,
So why do the teachers,
Set out just to annoy me.

Wiliam Joseff Davies (11)
Ysgol Brynhyfryd

THE FIRST DAY AT HIGH SCHOOL

I woke up very nervous but excited,
I got dressed and walked downstairs.
Ate my breakfast
ran back upstairs to get my bag,
watched TV for half an hour,
grabbed a packet of crisps,
said goodbye to everyone,
ran out of the door.

I felt so nervous I thought
I had real butterflies tingling
inside my stomach trying to
make me nervous.
I walked into next-door's garden
to meet my cousin, we felt sick,
we wanted to curl up into bed
and never come out.

We walked into the shop
to get some sweets, walked
very slowly hoping to miss
the school bus but we
did not miss it at all.
Everyone was waiting
silently for the bus.
We waited for ages
but after being nervous
and stupid about going to school
the bus did not come to pick us up,
so we jumped into my grandad's car
and made it to school so I would not
miss the school meeting.

Louise Francis (11)
Ysgol Brynhyfryd

SCHOOL

(On the phone) I will meet you
and four other people
by the white door.
Rushing to school brushing my teeth,
jumping into the car,
nothing can be wrong now!
Running to the white door,
no one was there!
I saw Ceri with some other girls,
I went to them and I walked into the school.
Masses of people, scared, noisy,
nice boys passing,
teachers, classes, where do I go?
Dinner . . . mmm . . . nice!
Time to go home,
back to school tomorrow.
Ahh! Help me!

Elan Evans (11)
Ysgol Brynhyfryd

MY FIRST DAY AT SCHOOL

Tuesday morning, 4th September!
My first day at Brynhyfryd.
We were the eldest in the primary
But now the youngest.
Feeling nervous but also excited.
Along came the taxi to pick me up.
A strange journey to school.
Everything so new.
New faces everywhere.
I walked nervously to the canteen
To meet the rest.
A room full of children
Chatting away.
In came the deputy to sort us out.
Off we went with our friendly form teacher.
Break time!
A river of children walking along
The bursting corridors.
The first bell rang.
We headed towards our classroom.
I was a bit lost
So I just followed the crowd.
So many teachers.
So many subjects
So many rooms.
Last bell!
Doors opening, children rushing out.
A long, tiring day but I survived.

Siôn Owen (11)
Ysgol Brynhyfryd

A First Trembling Day At Secondary School

Nervous, small, uncomfortable, brushed hair
New uniform, bag packed and washed teeth.
Pens rattling inside their cases.
Shoes spotless, not a mark on them, black socks,
Green jumpers, green skirt I look like a green snake!
All my nerves are churning up.

Which pen shall I use?
What bus am I on?
Will I meet new friends?
Will the teachers be nice?
Fat chance!
All my nerves are churning up.

Classroom, lessons, teachers, books,
Homework, form, swipe cards, lost
Chit-chatting between lessons,
Working as hard as you can,
Big buildings, so many rooms
All my nerves are churning up.

Plain muffin with melted chocolate on top,
Chips, donuts, fruit, salad, sausage rolls.
School dinners.
Everyone is big
And I'm hoping that the ground will swallow me.
All my nerves are churning up.
I see it coming; it's the top of the bus, my bus.
It's coming closer and closer and . . . gone!
Yes, gone to the distance without a twitch toward us,
Yes, it's gone without me chatting cosily on it.
Oh! Looks like I won't have to go to school today!

Ffiona Mair Jones (11)
Ysgol Brynhyfryd

SCHOOL

Hair brushing,
Bag sorting,
Showering,
Shoe polishing,
This is hard,
Very confusing.

I get to school.
Who are all these weird people?
Help!
I'm gonna cry,
No! This is high school.

I've calmed down now
My friends are here.
I love this school.

Ceri Eagle (11)
Ysgol Brynhyfryd

First Day At Secondary School

Children rushing,
Teachers lecturing,
Me, well I was lost.

The big white building of the school
Looking down at me,
An eleven-year-old girl with no idea where to go.
Minutes felt like hours.
Nobody to talk to or laugh and crack a joke.
Just me and the big white building!

The bell. Oh no! Panic! Panic!
Just remember:
Sir not Mr,
Miss not Mrs.
Sit down, no stand up!
Bonjour! Bore da! Hello!
Ermm . . . ermm!
Help!

First lesson.
Signing books, calling your name.
Teachers setting you up to make friends!
Everything's so different.
Oh no!
What if I make a mistake?
What if I get into trouble
On my first day?

Tick-tock, tick-tock! Ti . . .
Brrrrrrr!
The home bell.
Home, it seems so far away.

My family,
I wonder what kind of day they had.
As different as mine?
I bet they weren't so nervous as me!

Beca Haf Parry (11)
Ysgol Brynhyfryd

THE SCHOOL

The school is an evil trap which swallows up people for the day,
And doesn't let them out until the very end.
It feeds on children and destroys them with an evil poison
                                        called knowledge.
Pesky annoyances called teachers lecture you day in and day out.
Beware of school!
Sometimes they will imprison you for longer.
In the jaws of school in a detention or an after school club.
The block is a huge towering giant with ten mouths which all hold kids.
Then in an hour they are swallowed and taken further
                                      into what lurks beneath.
But what does this monster do?
It gives you a horrible thing!
It is known as an education.
In all humanity what kind of torture is that?

Daniel Brixey (13)
Ysgol Brynhyfryd

SCHOOL

School time again!
As I arrive on the bus
I see people being drawn inside
As if the school is a Venus flytrap
The doors, like leaves, slam shut.

Swallowing them whole
Engulfing everyone!

For hour after hour the pupils are stuck
Slowly being digested by acid-like teachers.
The school keeps on fighting, trying to hold them in
Drones on and on, not giving up
It wants its dinner,
It is starving.

And just when it's about to make the kill
It gives up and lets go . . .
Out come the flies from the holes
They are safe again for another day
Till tomorrow anyway!

Sam Shillito (12)
Ysgol Brynhyfryd

The Bell

There goes the bell for break,
There goes the bell for dinner time,
There goes the long-awaited bell for half term.
Streams of pupils flushing down every path of the school,
Rushing and pushing to get home.
But then it all goes to a sudden stop
When all the loud buses have gone,
All the teachers are alone,
But will be accompanied again soon.

Eilir Wyn Roberts (11)
Ysgol Brynhyfryd

First Day At School

First day at school,
I ask my sister for the way,
But she says no because,
She's the boss,
I went to the corridors,
I thought I heard the bell,
I saw my mates,
And asked them for help.

At registration,
The teacher was
Strict but helpful.
The bell went,
It was dinner time.
Big queues everywhere
Everyone hungry.

Books, books everywhere,
Each one wants covering.

Finally the bell rang,
Time to go home
And get ready for tomorrow.

Clwyd Edwards (11)
Ysgol Brynhyfryd

SCHOOL

Getting ready in the morning,
Knowing a whole school day is ahead of you.
The bell rings,
Crowds of children walking inside like a herd of wildebeest.
Registration, how boring.
The bell goes for the first lesson.
The teacher blabbering on about work.
Work, the worst thing in the world.
Second lesson, walking to another classroom.
Horrible hard chips,
Squishy vegetables,
Burnt sausages.
How disgusting, school dinners.
The bell goes, again
Registration, again,
Fourth lesson,
Fifth lesson,
At last home.

Alan Armstrong (11)
Ysgol Brynhyfryd

SCHOOL

School's going to be *boring*
School's too big
Schools have too many *children*

Going on the bus is *embarrassing*
Going to school is *scary*
Going to school is *a new start*

Work is hard
Work is too hard
Work is far too hard

Teachers, are they strict?
Teachers, are they tall?
Teachers, are they spooky?

*Boys' school
Form room,
Form teacher's make-up.*

Which form room is mine?

**Sioned Roberts (11)
Ysgol Brynhyfryd**

SCHOOL

I walked down the hill and saw a bunch of children.
There was some of them that I already knew
But I didn't talk to them,
I just wish I still had the flu,
I got on the bus and sat with my brother,
I was talking to him and a few of the others.

Then I got off the bus, wondering where to go
I saw my friend and stood with him.
I asked a woman where to go,
She shouted and said, 'To the canteen'.
We went to the canteen
There was no where to sit.

We stood very quiet and waited,
They started to talk about some stuff,
And they told us what form we were in,
A man told us to follow two women,
So that's what I did.
Up, up and up we went to the top of the stairs,
And then we sat down all in pairs.

It was a long day,
But then *dring, dring*,
And it was time to go,
Yes! We all shouted as we got on the bus,
And went home making no fuss.

Iestyn Jones (11)
Ysgol Brynhyfryd

FIRST DAY AT SCHOOL

Ready for school,
Looking cool,
Let's give it a bash,
Oooh!
I might have bangers and mash!

Why am I so small?
And everyone is so tall?
Why do I not fit in?
But everyone else
Like sardines in a tin!

The teachers really
Aren't that bad,
But some of them
Get a bit mad,
Why do I hate school,
Everyone else is acting cool,
I would rather
Be at home
With my brother
And my mother.

I can't wait till school finishes,
But then I'll come home and do the dishes.

Wil Sharp (11)
Ysgol Brynhyfryd

CLUBBING

Get in the club.
To get in on,
Start dancing to your favourite song.

Watching people all around,
Getting dizzy,
From the sound.

On the dance floor feeling fine,
DJ shouts,
'Let's have a good time,'
Makes people want,
Want to dance,
You couldn't stop if you had the chance.

Feeling funky,
Feeling fine,
Getting ready to sing that rhyme.

Getting sweaty,
Feeling hot,
But you know that you can't stop,
All your mates dancing round,
Getting dizzy from the sound.

Nearly at the dead of night,
But we're still raving to the flashing lights.

It's midnight,
Lights fade away,
Out to the streets,
You make your way.

Back to life,
Back to your zone,
Back to the place,
Back to the place you call your home.

Emily Freeman (12)
Ysgol Brynhyfryd

LONER

Do you see the girl, trying to hide?
Hiding her hurt, hiding her pride
The popular ones, don't care no more
Push her aside, she knows the score

Accepted once, forgotten now
Passers-by, just raise their brow
They've taunted, they've teased
Till their mocking, has ceased.

Do you see the hurt? Do you see the pain?
That's fixed upon her face again.
She hides behind her daily lies
Of 'I don't care, I don't mind'

Their words are bound to cause her pain
When they insult her over again
Her tears flow fast and free
But no one will stop and see

You're just like her, she's just like you
Can't you see she's got feelings too?
It really wouldn't take a while
To look at her and spread a smile

But still she stays, trying to hide
Hiding her hurt, hiding her pride
While the popular ones care no more
Push her aside and she knows the score.

Charlotte Masters (15)
Ysgol Brynhyfryd

THE CHOCOLATE BAR

I passed a sweet shop window
while walking home.
In that window was a big bar of chocolate.
It was just screaming for me to eat it . . .
'Go on, go on,
you know you want to!'
I shouldn't . . . I couldn't . . .
I won't . . . oh . . . alright.

I rushed into the shop,
bought that chocolate, my mouth watering
as I took off the shiny, purple wrapper
off it came.

I broke a bit of the smooth brown,
gorgeous chocolate,
started eating it . . .
mmm . . .
it's gorgeous,
it's fab,
it's tasty,
it's breath-taking,
it's . . . gone!

Emma Braid (12)
Ysgol Brynhyfryd

GHOST TRAIN

It roars on the track
as it comes closer and closer.
Lights that dazzle you like
a swarm of fireflies.
A whistle like a squealing monkey
that is in danger.
Closer and closer it comes
your heart pounding like a deer
getting chased by a tiger.
As it passes you feel as if you
are in a tornado
and then silence . . .

Sara Bowler (12)
Ysgol Brynhyfryd

THE STRUGGLE

As I walk through the streets in my head
I see a man searching for somewhere to lie for the night.
I feel his pain, his anger, his suffering,
I see his life as he does,
As one eternal struggle.
His life is nothing but a fight,
A fight he cannot win yet still he tries.
He's punched, hit, knocked out, for tonight
This is where he lies
Here he will try to survive.
He'll then wake tomorrow open his eyes and
Thank the Lord that he is alive!
But until then he's alone with his mind
Searching, not knowing what he'll find,
All this I cannot watch for much longer.
Compared to me he's so much stronger
I pull myself out of the streets in my head
Then I walk upstairs to my own warm bed.

Becky Challinor (15)
Ysgol Brynhyfryd

THE PASSING MOTORBIKE

At the end of the blistering road
a black speck grows
and its buzz grows louder.
The grass looks up, startled from its sleep.
A single light appears through the gloom
darting round the corners.
Buzzing loudly, leaving a trail
of polluted fog in its wake.
Closer and closer the blinding light comes . . .

Zoom

It buzzes past me at tremendous speed,
the light flickers into a red one
and disappears over the hill.
Silent again is the land, waiting for the day.

Ben Mcleod (12)
Ysgol Brynhyfryd

THROUGH THE EYES OF A CHILD

The night sky,
Bloodied by incessant bombing.
I crouch and cower
Like a caged animal
Praying, hoping to survive
Until the break of dawn.

With the light of day
Scars clutter the countryside,
Mud buildings flattened.
And in open fields
Yellow packages,
Presents from above
Charity by day
Attackers by night.

I am caught
In a spiral of terrorism,
Caught,
Entangled in a web of hatred.

Ffion Medi (15)
Ysgol Brynhyfryd

The Autumn Of Terror

As the cheerfulness of summer fades,
The beauty of autumn
Starts with a terrible blow
In America.

The air full of screams,
Like the wind blowing through naked trees,
As dust and rubble falls,
The first leaf floats to the ground.

Flames dance,
Red and yellow leaves flying in the wind,
The towers fall, arms outstretched,
Like two huge oak trees coming to an end.

As people collect bodies,
Animals collect food,
As the cities fall still with shock,
Forests fall quiet with sleep.

Huw Woodward (12)
Ysgol Brynhyfryd

SEPTEMBER 11TH 2001

On September the eleventh,
The world was struck with grief,
When terrorists
Killed thousands for their belief.
The destruction was incredible,
After the Twin Towers fell,
Leaving the area smoking,
Like an unimaginable hell.
People panicked and ran,
Others cowered in fear,
As the sirens started,
Sirens many would never hear.
People were buried in rubble,
As firemen tried to dig them out,
Many dying people,
Without hope, tried to shout.
But now there are no more survivors,
And America is ready to strike back,
But we hope for less to die,
For the morals the terrorists lack.

Owen Mills (13)
Ysgol Brynhyfryd

TERROR TOWERS

How they stood so straight and tall
How impressive they looked
Minutes is all they took to fall
Hundreds of families wrecked

How can people justify such an act
To take another human's life isn't right.
The rest of the world needs to make a pact
We know it isn't good to fight.

People need to feel safe and sure
About this sort of terrorist attack
We all know that there's is no quick cure
But we can't allow this terror to ever come back.

The clouds of billowing dust
The cries of horror and disbelief
The searching, searching from dawn till dusk
The finding of a loved one is such a relief

No one's life will be the same again
How can these people justify their cause
How can they create so much misery and pain
People should abide by the humanity laws.

Everyone should have freedom
Surely that's our God given right
Be allowed to roam our own kingdom
The Statue of Liberty, New York's ray of light.

Mathew Edge (13)
Ysgol Brynhyfryd

September 11th

Innocence, standing tall
Death and hatred as they fall.
Terror from the skies above
Grief and shock and death of love.
Suicide bombers from the air
Bring the death, without a care,
Metal, broken glass rains down
Smoke of black and grey and brown.
People jumping from the towers,
Flame erupting like Hell's flowers.
But now we think we should strike back
With ships and bombs and land attack,
But should we really stoop as low
To follow the path the terrorists go?

Tom Potter (14)
Ysgol Brynhyfryd

CANDLES

The Twin Towers hopelessly in suspense,
Like two candles in the wind,
As the gust came near.

Crash!
What a sight,
The plane struck like the wind,
People feel in fright.

As the fire extended,
The candles started to melt,
And their occupants,
Who knows how they felt?

Tears in the people's eyes,
Fell like many innocent lives,
With all their hard work through the year,
And as quickly as that they disappear.

The candles came down with fear,
They knew the end was near,
But a little girl came to sight,
And made darkness come to light.

Robert Steffan Parry (12)
Ysgol Brynhyfryd

WHY?

Two solid pillars
Cascading to the ground.
Bodies jumping, falling,
Screaming and shouting.
Terror and panic,
Lives destroyed,
Innocent people
Crushed in the ruins.
Helpless searchers,
Praying and hoping
For any survivors.
The President and people
Look on in tragic despair
As the astounding news
Shakes the world . . .
Why?

Elin Morgan (14)
Ysgol Brynhyfryd

GROUND ZERO

Stunned, shocked, unable to believe
A message of hate so hard to receive
Death and destruction come out of the sky
A nation in mourning wondering why

Hijack, violence, a telephone plea
No one quite knowing what was to be
Fire, smoke, before they came down
New York had lost its Twin Tower crown

Panic, bravery, heroes of the day
Thanksgiving from those who got away
Hope, prayer, replaced by grief
The world looked on in disbelief

Revenge, attack,
The need to strike back
Think, wait,
Nothing's won by hate

Watching, waiting, the nations decide
Terrorism must have no place it can hide
Power, oppression, a people in despair
The needs of the poor, does anyone care?

Bombs, warships, missiles cruise
This is a war the USA dare not lose
But what of the outcome? What about peace?
A hope for the future where all fighting will cease.

Bethan Rowlands (15)
Ysgol Brynhyfryd

SEPTEMBER 11TH

A cry of shock
As the cameras click,
Tears fall
Like autumn leaves.

A cry of grief
As news reporters speak,
Darkness gathers
Like winter days.

A cry of disbelief
As the towers fall,
Crumble, perish
Like the last roses of summer.

A cry of loneliness
In the ruins,
Like an orphan lamb
Who's lost his mother.

Heledd Fflur Morgan (12)
Ysgol Brynhyfryd

WHY?

Why?
Just a normal day
With nothing sad at all
Until the impact
The world pauses
And all look at America
Why?
Just a normal day . . .
But at nine
The world stops.

Just a normal day . . .
What? Who? Why?
Was it a mistake?
Did the plane lose control?
Who would do such a thing?
What did *we* do?

Just a normal day?
As debris scatters the land
Like rain of gloom and despair
Bodies fall like tears
Before the pillars crumble.

Lowri Stubbs (12)
Ysgol Brynhyfryd

MOTHER

No matter where you go,
No matter what you do . . .
All the love I have to give
Goes right along with you.

Mother . . .
As a beacon in my life . . .
Through all my trials
And triumphs
Your love has shined so bright.

There's no love
Like my mother's love
And I know that it is true . . .
Every time my mother smiles
Her love comes shining through.

As a mother
You have always been
So sweet in every way
My precious gift from heaven
Bringing heartfelt love each day.

When I think about you Mother
A picture comes to mind . . .
A woman sweet and gentle
With a heart,
That's one of a kind.

Cathryn Jones (11)
Ysgol Brynhyfryd

ONE WISH

I stare at a lonesome star that shines,
Shining through the night,
Answering dreams of many
With a magic ray of light.

But when I have a dream of love
To brighten up my days
The star fades into darkness
And a voice within me says,
'You cannot fix your problems
By reaching to the sky,
Because love will come to you,
And those who wait
Will have it till they die'.

So then I close my curtains
Not feeling much at ease,
For I have waited long enough
To find a love to seize.

They say it's better to have loved and lost
Than to have never loved at all
So I'm prepared to take a chance
When Cupid decides to call.

Emma Jones (15)
Ysgol Brynhyfryd

THE LAKE

Softly the pale moon shines full
on the surface of the glassy lake,
ripples disturb the surface
as koi carp leap to pay homage to the moon,
glinting silver.

Black cat paws its way softly to the lake,
stops, sniffs the air.
Pigeons disturbed, fly up to the sky,
black cat watches, spellbound,
time freezes.

At the paling of the sky
distant breezes dance amongst
the tall tops of beech trees,
trees which bend to whisper their secrets to one other.
Dawn breaks.

Lauren Gledhill (15)
Ysgol Brynhyfryd

EVERY ROSE HAS THORNS

She held the rose in her pale hands
and caressed its smooth soft skin,
she thought of best laid plans
but she also thought of sin.

He gave her the rose on that night
after they had danced upon a cloud
they came across the passing rainbow
and danced onwards, feeling proud.

And when the time arrived
for the rain storm to attack
they danced in the storm's falling gifts
as clouds too, have tears they can't hold back.

But she also knew that all things change
that every rose has thorns,
and her tears, to began to fall
gun in hand she felt hopelessly torn.

She lay the rose upon her chest,
felt its presence as she cried,
together they had danced upon a cloud
and together they wilted and died.

Jane Hesketh (15)
Ysgol Brynhyfryd

SEASONS

As one season comes and another one goes
just like winter with its freezing snows.
As winter thaws we move into spring,
once more this life begins this eternal thing.
The birds start to whistle and the leaves begin to grow
as the days pass away then the colours start to show.
Summer comes on a warm, blue sky day,
can sometimes last for ages or quickly fade away.
But whatever she has to offer and whatever she may decide
our hearts will be filled with laughter and our memories
                              will never be denied.
Winds sweeps like a new broom,
autumn is upon us so soon,
everywhere is yellow and everywhere is brown.
Everything that was, now lays dead on the ground
soon it will be winter and the snows will come
and once more again the seasons will be done.

Zara Blain (14)
Ysgol Dinas Brân

THE OLD MAN

Swirls of mist in the gathering gloom
Dragons breathing fire, men wielding blades
Goblins and trolls in the night dark as shadows
Hippogriffs roaming in the night

The town people in their homes
Shiver and quiver like mice being faced with a cat
They are worried that the monsters
Would take them away

But then a man hooded black like shadows
His eyes twinkling
His face white like a ghost
Waving his wand in a flash of light, the creatures disappear.

Timothy Knibbs (11)
Ysgol Dinas Brân

THE GREEN MEAN KILLING MACHINE

He is a green mean killing machine!
Slowly, slowly his evil eyes open.
He unfolds his bat-like wings.
He emerges.
Dragon of fiery Hell springs to life.
His talons gripping his prey at terrifying speed.
Just his stare can kill his foe.

Philip Pybus (11)
Ysgol Dinas Brân

THE CREATURES OF THE EARTH

The graceful creatures of the earth;
So beautiful and so tranquil
All getting on with their own little lives
Not trying to take over the world
Oh if only we were like that
Then the world would be a much happier place

From elephants to goldfish
From tigers to dolphins
So all individual in their own little ways
Precious and special
They all are so content

A lion is not just a lion
A bird is not just a bird
They all have feelings just like us
So let's altogether put a stop to all harm
And distress to these harmless creatures
Leave them alone and they'll do no damage

Would you go round shooting
People of your own kind?
Would you murder a friend of yours or mine?
No
Well, don't kill the animals
Leave them alone
Don't torture these innocent friends
They've done nothing to us.

If you would like to help
To help put a stop to this murdering of animals
Then join the RSPCA
Or RSPB if your love is for birds
These helpful charities will inform you what you can do
To play your part
In the bid to stop cruelty to animals.

Joanne Morris (14)
Ysgol Dinas Brân

BROKEN AND BLIND

As I sit here alone
In a depressed state of mind,
Darkness is upon me
I'm broken and blind.

Insane, obsessive I know
But I never believed
I'd be the one to let go

I feel nothing
People feel nothing for me
Oblivious to humanity
Black, black is all I see.

I don't exist now
You let me fall
I was choked and chained
Now I hate you all.

I still sit alone,
Out of my mind
Darkness is upon me
I'm broken and blind.

Adam Rogers (16)
Ysgol Dinas Brân

WALES

To live in Wales is to be conscious of . . .
The sun rising above the towering mountains
As the snow on the peaks slowly disappear, until they look bare.
To hear the national anthem, ringing in our ears.
We listen proudly.
The Welsh dragon on our country's flag stands and stares
To frighten off anybody who dares to intrude.
We see all of the famous Welsh people doing their jobs,
Letting us know every day to thank the Lord that we are Welsh.
Though we moan about the foul weather,
The rain drizzling down the double-glazed pane of glass
Wales itself is a glowing sun,
Providing light and happiness for Welsh people.

Kay Rowley (14)
Ysgol Dinas Brân

AN UNFINISHED POEM

If this world was perfect we'd all be free
Living in paradise and harmony
Everyone with a smile upon their face
The world would be a better place
Without anger, pain or greed
Whatever their race, colour or creed
Nobody hungry, sad and cold
Everyone growing up to be old.

Alex Bebbington (14)
Ysgol Dinas Brân

MAGIC

Mysterious-looking cats,
comfy magical hats.

Flying on brooms above the sky light,
it was a mysterious dark night, as dark as coal.

A vanishing cloak,
the owls had awoke.

Prowling through thick dark woods,
Where the ugly cats stood.

The cunning owl swooped past.
Whoosh, through the sky night.

Merlin's black and white wand
as long as a branch.

Flying brooms all day long.

Nakita Furmage (11)
Ysgol Dinas Brân

FOOTBALL MATCH

Blood-red crowd
Playing like lions
Players charge, rhinos in battle
Wind howling wolfishly
Crowd chant support
Managers scream instructions
Wingers run like sprinters
Scoreline expectations
Crowd disappointment
Teams unsatisfied.

William Eastwood (11)
Ysgol Dinas Brân

THE BRIGHT LIFE

In a place I've been, there is no dark,
At night the sky is pink,
Even blackboards are not black.
When it rained the rain was green,
And the clouds a shocking shade of red,
Inside caves there was an orange glow
And coal was a beautiful sky blue.
All this bright colour was lovely,
But I couldn't quite take it all in,
When I closed my eyes I saw rainbows,
And suddenly seeing black would be a dream,
So I came back to the land of dullness,
Where the sky is constantly grey,
Nowhere I looked was bright,
But I visit the land of nice colours,
When I sleep in my bed at night.

Susie Davies (14)
Ysgol Dinas Brân

TERROR IN AMERICA

People going to work, just another normal day,
Little did they know the terror on its way,
Aeroplanes into the Trade Center flew.
Smoke, fire, screaming, what should they do?

Thousands of innocent people have lost their lives,
To the violent hijackers in the skies,
Does anyone know exactly what has gone on?
Lots of people are lost, maybe gone.

Clouds of ash down every street,
People hoping their families they will soon meet.
Will they ever get over this terrible nightmare,
Will they understand the reality and the despair?

Bethan Richards (14)
Ysgol Dinas Brân

SCHOOL

The bell rings,
School begins
Gum and graffiti sprawled across our book
Here comes that punishing look,

Lesson by lesson the day goes by,
Children's brains become empty and dry.
At last, break arrives,
This is one thing which helps us survive.

More lessons follow,
When will anyone hear our sorrow,
Maths, science, Welsh and English,
In the end this is what will finish us.

The bell rings, lunch is here,
Books and teachers stay well clear.
Children play,
While teachers lock themselves away.

Two lessons to go,
Brain cells are now on low.
Five past three and we pack away,
Forget all that you learnt today.

Forget the work and your sorrows
That is until tomorrow.

Emma Watson (14)
Ysgol Dinas Brân

DREAM ON!

I want to fly into the sky,
Above the clouds and trees,
I want to drift along the shore,
Guided by the breeze.

I want to step on golden sands,
Beneath the golden sun,
I want to do so many things,
But for now I'll just . . .
Dream on!

Natalie Astle (14)
Ysgol Dinas Brân

AUTUMN LEAVES

The leaves in autumn
begin to fall,
stark and bare
are the trees so tall.

You can see your breath
the days are so cold,
everything is sleeping,
yet another year old.

Bonfires and fireworks
we come to know,
until autumn is replaced
by the winter snow.

Paul Brown (14)
Ysgol Dinas Brân

MONSTERS

Under my bed lives a monster called Fred,
who is small, green and fat with a black bowler hat
and a gold rimmed monocle.
Fred is a monster who's really quite calm,
he's well educated and has lots of charm.
He doesn't eat kids or scare them for fun,
he would much rather watch Corrie with a burger and bun.
Fred likes science and maths which is really quite cool,
because now I've found someone who can help me
with homework from school.
He doesn't like English, geography as well,
he quite often says, 'Maps and Shakespeare should go to Hell!'
Fred and me play after school every day,
and after that we go to watch a movie.
Mum likes Fred and Fred likes Mum,
she says he's like a cuddly green son.
At bedtime we have a super treat,
and then we curl up and Fred sleeps by my feet.

Lee Jones (14)
Ysgol Dinas Brân

THE FLOWER

The little flower was small and red,
and it sat all lonely in the bed.

No one ever came to see
except the orange bumblebee.

Then one day it grew and grew,
and soon the whole village knew.

The flower that used to be small,
had now become so very tall.

Now it's gone beyond the wall,
we share it with everyone and all.

Hannah Green (14)
Ysgol Dinas Brân

MY SCHOOL

My school is a magic school,
and my friends can transfigurate things,
but I can't,
all I do is sit around and watch them.

The corridors are as windy as spaghetti,
twisting and turning,
the classrooms are as dark as night,
and the teachers are as jolly as clowns.

Geraint Lloyd (11)
Ysgol Dinas Brân

SPACE

What would space be like?
Space would be a black hole in the sky,
With lots of shining stars,
Space is like a black blanket
With shiny things like stars,
Up high in space the moon lives,
There might be aliens or even monsters,
There might be rocks,
Big ones and small ones,
There might be different animals,
Different kinds of things,
Space might be dark and scary,
Bright and beautiful
Or ugly and horrible.
What do you think space is like?

Amy May Derbyshire-Styles (11)
Ysgol Dinas Brân

MY BEST FRIEND

Sometimes we argue,
Sometimes we fight,
I know she's always there for me -
Even alone at night.

Some things we share,
Some things we won't,
I know she's always looking out for me
Even if I don't.

Someone says one thing,
Someone says another.
I know she's always truthful to me,
She's like another brother.

Somebody's mean to me,
Somebody's nice to me,
I know she's always my best friend -
Well . . . that's as far as I can see.

Holly Cottrell (14)
Ysgol Dinas Brân

THE TIGER

Its tail is a long rope
Used for balance.
Its stripes are as black as night
Used for camouflage.
Its big staring eyes
Used for sight.
Its claws are lethal weapons
Used for attacking
And its deadly teeth as sharp as knives
Used for . . . devouring.

Luke Smith (11)
Ysgol Dinas Brân

NIGHT IN THE CITY

The moon was glistening brightly,
before he decided to play hide and seek.
The cars were roaring madly,
shooting round and round like rockets.
The shops were as silent as space,
inside nothing to be heard except the squeak of a little mouse.
The only person to be seen was the little old man
walking his dog slowly down the road.
The dog barked like he had seen the ghost of the city.
The lamps were staring down at the mice on the road
like a dragon looking at his prey.
And out of the blue a light came up from the sky slowly.
The lamps went dull and went to sleep,
the shops started to light up and fill up with noisy people
from the little silent man and his dog.
As all these changes happen slowly night turns into day.

Dawn Morrison (11)
Ysgol Dinas Brân

STORM AND SUN

His wavy hair, his flashing eyes,
Remind me so of stormy skies,
Her golden hair, her warm green eyes,
Remind me so of clear blue skies.

His locks conceal a mind of pride,
In none but her does he confide,
Her beauty's light and does not dim,
But all herself she saves for him.

He is tall and dark and strong,
She is pale, her hair is long,
His brawn is tough but it will fall,
To her, the beauty of them all,
Her heart beats strong but it will yield,
To him, with feelings all concealed.

They live in a world away from others,
Hand in hand they walk like brothers,
Skies of silver, fields of gold,
As in their hearts their love unfolds,
A love like none that's gone before,
Their love will burn strong evermore.

Storm and Sun are joined together,
Blowing strong they'll shine forever.

Nicola Fleck (13)
Ysgol Emrys Ap Iwan

MAN OF THE SEAS

He scrapes up and down the coastline,
guided only by the commands of the moon.
His emotions can change
from a chaotic bombardment of violent wrath
to a calm, pallid, languid laze,
that disturbs nobody, only soothes.

His briney breath alerts anybody of his presence,
his twisted, tangled, straggles of beard and hair
are represented by seaweed and kelp.

He oversees a dark, secluded, predatory realm
ruled by savage hunters.
But, like his own personality, there is also
a light, beautiful community living in peace,
undisturbed by the world above the waves.

His face, sometimes decorated with sea-foam,
mirrors and imitates the sky, his older brother.

He will remain this way until the end,
slowly harbouring the waves
and harvesting the bounty of his domain.
Watching the rise and fall of civilizations
that may have met him upon his stormy waters and ragged coasts.
They may have even tried unlocking some of his hidden secrets.

Jamie Blythin (14)
Ysgol Emrys Ap Iwan

My Everything

What is she, my little everything?
And all that is somehow nothing,
An innocent being that cannot comprehend,
Cannot possibly comfort me in my hours of need.
Will I ever know her gratitude?
She is the all that has robbed me of my dignity,
offering nothing in return.
How can I adore my everything so?
I know that it is bizarre to love a selfish one so selflessly,
To live for one that cannot speak your name . . .
But I sigh and I watch as my little everything slumbers peacefully,
And I am enchanted once again.
Will I ever break this spell?
This curse that my everything has bestowed upon me.
Will she always be my everything?
I feel so useless,
I cradle my everything close,
I want to guard her from the world,
Protect her from pain and anguish and keep her always in my arms.
But instead I sigh and I watch,
As my daughter, my little everything, slumbers peacefully.

Samantha Strauch (15)
Ysgol Emrys Ap Iwan

MAYBE

That lad walks by,
He smiles and waves,
Hair as brown as wood,
Eyes as blue as skies.

I feel queasy, could it be love?
He stops and talks nearby,
The butterflies in my stomach clearly states that it could,
He walks by, I blush and he asks me why.

I didn't answer, my mind going blank,
What was the question?
I could've hit myself with a plank!
I sadly realised he had gone, thinking I wouldn't see him again.

I walked along the corridor,
His bright blue eyes still in my head,
It had gone wrong, like the times before,
I wanted to go home back to my warm bed.

Around the corner, I would be in class,
As I turned, I hoped to see him again,
My heart broken, I wandered into class,
I saw him stare, his blue eyes through the glass.

My heart skipped a beat,
He smiled and waved,
I flickered my blue-green eyes
At the way he behaved.

Lesson had finished - hip, hip, hooray,
He wandered over to me,
I wouldn't see him for two days,
He gave me a surprise.

He kissed me; I was on cloud nine,
He said bye and turned away,
At that moment I knew it wouldn't be long before he was mine!
I had to run, before I was late!

Louise Kirk (13)
Ysgol Emrys Ap Iwan

MY DOG MAC

My dog Mac is a real cool dude,
He likes to 'pig out' on lots of food.

Oh me, oh my, he thinks he can fly,
For he chases the seagulls that swoop by.

As for *cats*, well what can I say,
He chases them every day.

He lets you in with a friendly paw,
But you'd better run when you head for the door.

When the telephone rings he's up with a spring,
Cos my dog Mac is a real nutty thing.

When it's time for *'walkies'* he's jumping and prancing,
He could be the next star of disco dancing.

He looks so cute when he's had his hair cut,
You'd never believe he was my little mutt.

As you can see he's a real little terror,
That's probably why he's a West Highland Terrier.

I love my dog Mac.

Jessica Whitehouse (13)
Ysgol Emrys Ap Iwan

MATHS, WHAT'S THE POINT?

Why's maths so hard
metric, imperial
metre and yard.
Maths, what's the point?

Pythagoras, wasn't he Greek?
$a^2+b^2=c^2$ - what does it mean?
In my mind there's a leak.
Maths, what's the point?

Percentage, decimal and fraction
it's just so hard
with me there's no action.
Maths, what's the point?

Shapes, how many are there?
3D, 2D, cubes and squares
do I care?
Maths, what's the point?

Inequalities and trigonometry
we take so long
the teacher has time for a cup of tea.
Maths, what's the point?

My worst subject is maths
why can't it be easy?
When I ask the teacher he just laughs.
Maths, what's the point?

James Longden (13)
Ysgol Emrys Ap Iwan

NATURE

Nature is a beautiful thing,
A lovely sight to see,
With trees and flowers,
You could stare for hours,
I wish it was made just for me.

Unbelievable colours,
With rain and sun they grow.
Every day we see nature,
I hope it doesn't go.

All the animals of the forest
Are setting out on duty,
Why can't we just do the same,
To protect our nature's beauty?

Stephen Marsh (13)
Ysgol Emrys Ap Iwan

WITHOUT YOU . . .

Without you dreams don't exist,
Without you classical music is missed.
Without you love is not true,
Without you cows don't moo.
Without you the world is a dump,
Without you my heart no longer pumps.
Without you my world is turned upside down,
Without you I feel like a clown.
Without you my words are just air,
I'm without you, it's just not fair.
Without you.

Hannah Watson (13)
Ysgol Emrys Ap Iwan

THE WATERS DEEP

They swim around and hunt all day,
and eat whatever comes their way.
They can see through the tiniest gaps,
and when they do their mouths go
> *Snap!*

The water's deep,
the sharks are thin,
the current's strong,
> *So come on in!*

Their teeth are sharp, just like a pin,
especially when a carp comes in.
One row above, one row beneath,
these are a shark's amazing teeth.

The water's deep,
the sharks are thin,
the current's strong,
> *So come on in!*

Jazmine Bonnell (13)
Ysgol Emrys Ap Iwan

WITHOUT YOU...

Without you the rain clouds will follow me everywhere,
Without you I would not be alive,
Without you I would not know you,
Without you I would not be able to go anywhere,
Without you my life would be a mess,
Without you I would never see night, just endless days,
Without you my life would be hell.

Daniel Constanzo (13)
Ysgol Emrys Ap Iwan

SPRING, SUMMER, AUTUMN AND WINTER

Spring is a time for a new start, for everybody and everything,
People and animals all start afresh.
Really the main thing in spring
Is the sheep which have newborns.
New lambs is what people think about in spring,
Growing up and becoming parents themselves.

Summer is totally different from spring,
Under the sun, catching a tan.
Mums and dads take their children to the beach,
More time in the sun to play more games.
Every beach is covered with deckchairs,
Red-hot and too hot to sit on.

Autumn is a change from sun to leaves,
Under the trees is a ground full of acorns.
The leaves are mixed together, red, brown and green,
Unless the road man cleans the street.
More leaves, conkers and acorns fall,
Not a child dares miss the games.

And all they have to do is find some string,
Not too long and not too short,
Dry the conkers from the vinegar and tie the string around.

Winter is here at last, just in time for Christmas,
In comes the snow and out go the leaves.
Now every girl and boy has left their milk and cookies,
Time to go and sleep tight and no peeping out the door.
Even when Santa comes, he will never eat all the cookies,
Round about 5am Christmas has reached us at last.

Christine Brough (13)
Ysgol Emrys Ap Iwan

WHEN THE SUN IS SHINING

When the sun is shining
it's hard to bear.
Some people say it's
not even there.

When the sun is shining
it's always in the air.
Sometimes even people
do a nice little prayer.

Some people say
you can even touch it.
Some people say you can't
because it's always in the air.

When the sun is shining
it's always very hot.
Some said because
it's always boiling hot.

When the sun is shining
it always goes in your eyes.
But every time the sun goes down
we always say goodbye.

Kieran Buser Evans (11)
Ysgol Emrys Ap Iwan

MY RABBIT

Maybe you've heard rumours about rabbits,
Like they've got big teeth and like carrots,
But between me and you this is not always true,
And it makes me feel rather embarrassed.

There's one certain rabbit I know of,
Who's real cute but a bit of a show-off,
He eats lots of stuff,
And he's covered in fluff,
And leaping around he is fond of.

Chester's the name of my bunny,
And some of his habits are funny,
He's strange for a rabbit, he won't eat his carrots,
And only comes out when it's sunny.

The reason for this I surmise,
Is that carrots are good for your eyes,
But because he won't eat them,
His peepers have weakened,
So glasses for him I must buy.

Liam Doyle (11)
Ysgol Emrys Ap Iwan